MOMS SAY THE
FUNNIEST THINGS!

MOMS SAY THE
FUNNIEST THINGS!

A Collection of Motherly Wit and Wisdom

BRUCE LANSKY

Illustration by Dave Allen

🅼 Meadowbrook Press
Distributed by Simon & Schuster
New York

Library of Congress Cataloging-in-Publication Data

Lansky, Bruce
Moms say the funniest things: a collection of motherly wit and wisdom/
Bruce Lansky.
  p. cm.
  ISBN: 0-88166-178-3
  1. Mothers—Humor. 2. American wit and humor. I. Title.
PN6231.M68L36 1991
818'.5407—dc20   90-26455
                                                CIP
Simon & Schuster Ordering #: 0-671-74183-7

Production Editor: Kerstin Gorham
Production Manager: Lynne Cromwell
Typographer: Jon Wright
Cover Illustration: Dave Allen

Published by Meadowbrook Press, 18318 Minnetonka Boulevard,
Deephaven, MN 55391.

BOOK TRADE DISTRIBUTION by Simon & Schuster, a division of Simon
and Schuster, Inc., 1230 Avenue of the Americas, New York, NY
10020.

96 95 94 93 6 5 4 3

Printed in the United States of America

ACKNOWLEDGMENTS

I want to thank the following people for their help in recalling the funny things their moms said to them:

Richard Pomazal
Ramona Czer
Jim Leba
Elizabeth Weiss
Kerstin Gorham

I also want to acknowledge Vicki Lansky's role in providing some of the material for this book. Vicki has used a number of the lines in this book on our children. One of her favorites is: "Because I'm the mother and I say so." That used to end most discussions, but now that our kids are teenagers, it doesn't work quite so well.

In particular I would like to acknowledge the contributions of Dr. Richard Pomazal, associate professor of marketing and management at Wheeling Jesuit College. Rick provided numerous gems from his childhood. Upon seeing his compiled list of quotes, Rick's mother replied: "Well, although he might not have *obeyed* me, this list indicates that he at least *listened*...." To Rick, his mother, and all mothers who have imparted their wisdom, thank you.

DEDICATION

I want to dedicate this book to my mother, Loretta. Mom played the mother role with great drama and intensity. She was a woman who wanted the very best for her five children. I remember with pleasure and/or dread some of her favorite expressions.

Mom's favorite proverb was "improve each shining hour." By that she meant that we should always be practicing our instruments, doing homework, or reading a book; not reading comics, watching TV, or fighting. When we got bored with improving ourselves, we used to wrestle, and the whole house would shake. Mom would charge up the stairs to break up the fracas, but she rarely succeeded. She took some consolation from the idea that we were at least "improving" our wrestling.

Mom used to hover in the halls between our rooms to determine whether we were practicing our instruments. If we weren't she'd say, "I don't hear you practicing," until she could hear my clarinet, my brothers' violin and trumpet, and my sister's flute. How she could stand the racket, I'll never know.

Because we practiced our wrestling a lot more than we practiced our musical instruments, all four boys wrestled in high school, and three wrestled in college—one in international competition. High school wrestling matches are very loud affairs, but when Mom came to them you could hear her voice above all the others screaming, "You can do it!" Usually, we did.

Mom wasn't much of a cook. Too bad microwave ovens and microwave dinners hadn't been invented when we were young. When we refused to eat some vegetable which, in addition to being green (and therefore yucky) was also burnt, she would say, "How do you know if you don't like it until you try it?" Believe me, we knew.

Mother's memory is fading, so she may not remember all the wonderful times we had together. But I want to let her know that somehow all the hard work she logged in trying to "improve" me seems to have worked (though my kids might not agree).

Thanks, Mom. I love you.

TABLE OF CONTENTS

You'll always be my little boy.

INTRODUCTION

Every mother has to get her children out of bed, dressed, cleaned up, fed, to school, fed again, cleaned up again, undressed, and back to bed again. Very few children go along with this routine voluntarily. When logic won't work and time and tempers are short, moms come up with some very funny lines to get their way.

Some of these lines make us laugh: "If God had wanted us to fool around, He would have given us the Ten Suggestions," and "You're lucky you're flat-chested; when you're sixty you won't sag into your soup."

And some of these lines make us groan and roll our eyes: "You can't fool me, I'm your mother. I have eyes in the back of my head," and "Make sure to wear clean underwear; you never know when you'll be in an accident."

In this book I've collected hundreds of wise, witty, and peculiar expressions and snappy comebacks that mothers throughout the ages have used to bail themselves out of almost every conceivable parenting problem. If you find some gems you'd like to add to your repertoire, remember that all these lines are more effective when delivered with a twinkle in your eye.

SECTION I:
DAILY RITUALS

THE WAKE-UP SERVICE

Rise and shine!

Time to get up!

How come I can hear your alarm clock in my bedroom and you're still asleep?

Remember, the early bird catches the worm.

If you're sick, you'll have to stay in bed all day— no TV.

Now get out of bed before I dump you out.

If you don't get dressed, I'll send you to school in your pajamas.

Make sure to wear clean underwear; you never know when you'll be in an accident.

How many days have you worn those socks?

Don't you have any jeans without holes in them?

Tuck your shirt into your pants.

Tie your shoelaces before you trip on them.

Hurry up or you'll be late for school.

You're slower than molasses in January.

Get the lead out of your pants.

Don't forget your books.

You'd forget your head if it weren't connected to your neck.

Remember to put on a happy face.

THE EDUCATOR

I'm sorry. Math wasn't my best subject, either.

What did you learn in school today?

What do you mean, "nothin"?

Don't they teach you anything?

I'm going to have a little talk with your teacher.

And if I find out you're not paying attention, I'll give you a lesson you'll never forget.

How much homework do you have?

Finish your homework, then you can go out and play.

No TV until you've done all your homework.

Don't answer that phone. It's not for you.

Hello. I'm sorry, she can't come to the phone.

Don't worry, it wasn't the White House calling to confer about the Middle East crisis.

What are you doing up at 12:00? It's way past your bedtime.

You'll have to finish your homework on the bus tomorrow morning.

When your teacher asks to see your homework, you'd better not tell her your grandfather died. You've already told her that. Twice.

If you spent half the time doing your homework that you spend making up excuses, you'd be an A student.

THE HYGIENIST

Cleanliness is next to Godliness, and if you don't wash
your hands this minute, you'll be even closer to God!

Wash up and help me set the table—dinner's in five minutes.

Where have you been? I called you for dinner a half an hour ago.

You heard me call you—all the kids in the neighborhood came in for dinner but you.

You snacked all day and now you're not hungry.

Let me see your hands.

You call that clean?

There must be millions of germs crawling around on your hands.

I could plant flowers in the dirt under those nails.

How many times do I have to tell you to wash your hands before dinner?

If I've told you once, I've told you a thousand times.

Get back in the bathroom and wash up.

Don't just wipe your hands on the towel, turn on the water.

Don't just run the water, put your hands in it.

Don't just put your hands in the water, wash them with soap.

And while you're at it, don't forget to wash behind your ears.

Hurry up. Your dinner's getting cold, and I'm getting hungry.

If you're not ready to eat in one minute, we're starting without you.

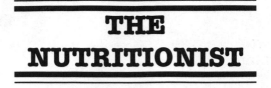

THE
NUTRITIONIST

Smell it, don't drool in it.

Come and get it!

If you're not at the table in one minute, I'm going to come and get you.

Let us say grace. Amen.

Now, get to work. I don't want to see any food left on your plate.

There's only one entree on the menu tonight, and you're going to like it.

Eat it—it's good for you.

It's a balanced meal—there are foods from every food group: yellow, green, white, and brown.

I'm not a short-order cook.

If you don't like what I cook, why don't *you* cook for the family?

When *you* buy the food in this house, then you can have pizza every day.

C'mon, try it—you just might like it.

Eat it—it won't kill you. I'm still alive.

How do you know you won't like it until you've tried it?

Who knows? Maybe spinach will turn out to be your favorite food.

It'll make you strong like Popeye.

Stop playing with your food.

Mashing your spinach with your fork won't make it disappear.

Don't roll your bread into little balls and throw them at your sister.

And stop blowing bubbles in your milk.

Stop fidgeting and sit still.

I told you not to eat a cookie just an hour before supper.

Now start eating. Your food is getting cold, and I'm getting angry.

You'd better eat your carrots, or you won't be able to see in the dark.

If you don't eat your green vegetables, you'll get rickets (or is it scurvy? I forget).

Fish is brain food. Maybe if you ate some, you'd understand what I'm talking about.

Think of all the starving children in Ethiopia, Afghanistan, Bangladesh, India, and China.

When I was a girl, I didn't let any food go to waste. I was a member of the "Clean Plate Club."

So what if I'm 20 pounds overweight. At least I didn't die of malnutrition.

If you don't eat your dinner, you won't get any dessert. And it just so happens that we're having your favorite dessert tonight.

No dessert for you tonight—don't say I didn't warn you.

I hope you dream about fish, spinach, carrots, and green beans, because that's what you're having for breakfast tomorrow.

MRS. SANDMAN

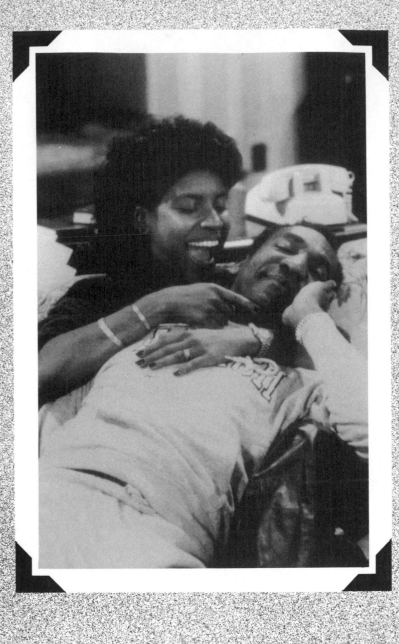

Now go upstairs, brush your teeth, get into your
pajamas, and then I'll tell you a story.

Time for bed, sleepyhead.

I thought I told you to get ready for bed.

Are you deaf, or am I losing my mind?

If you're in bed when I come in to say good night,
I'll read you a story.

And if you're not in bed, you're in big trouble.

Stop jumping on your beds and put down those
pillows. You'll get so worked up you'll never fall
asleep.

Now settle down and say your prayers.

You know what comes after "Now I lay me down to
sleep." You say it every night.

We only have time for a very short story.

Once upon a time . . . and they all lived happily
ever after.

OK, lights out.

Sorry, no more stories.

Good night, sleep tight, and don't let the bedbugs bite.

OK, I'll get you another drink of water, but you'd better not wet your bed.

There are no ghosts under your bed. We called in the Ghostbusters last night.

I don't want to hear another peep from you. Good night for the last time.

If I hear one more sound, I'll send your father upstairs.

What are you doing out of bed?

If you're not back in bed by the time I count to ten, you'll be sorry.

Honey, please go upstairs and put your children to sleep. I'm bushed.

SECTION II:
DON'T MESS AROUND
WITH MOM

THE BOSS

Are you deaf? If you're not already, you soon will be.

When your mother talks, you listen.

Now clean the wax out of your ears so you can hear what I'm telling you.

Read my lips.

Don't you dare talk to your mother in that tone of voice.

Don't shout; I'm not deaf.

Don't interrupt me when I'm lecturing you.

Because.

Because I'm your mother and I said so.

And I'll be your mother until the day I die.

If you know what's good for you, you'll do what I say.

If you don't like it, you can go up to your room and sulk.

I've made my decision, and you're going to live with it.

My decision is maybe, and that's final.

No ifs, ands, or buts.

If it's OK with your father, it's OK with me. But don't tell him I said it was OK with me.

THE SCOLD

You should know better than that.

Act your age, not your shoe size.

What has gotten into you?

Sorry, that doesn't cut the mustard with me.

This is where I draw the line.

I don't care if all your friends' parents let them do it on national TV.

You'd better watch your step.

You're skating on thin ice.

You're getting too big for your britches.

Get down off your high horse.

Don't get smart with me, or pretty soon your backside will smart.

Don't bite the hand that feeds you.

Don't bite the hand that pays your allowance, either.

Someday you'll get yours.

You'll get married and have a child just like you.

THE DETECTIVE

Just where do you think you're going?

You can't fool me, I'm your mother.

I wasn't born yesterday.

I didn't fall off a turnip truck, either.

I've got eyes in the back of my head.

I have a sixth sense—call it woman's intuition.

I always know when you're up to no good, even if I'm miles away.

Something's wrong.

It's too quiet in the kitchen.

OK, who ate all the brownies?

Don't all answer at once.

You know I have ways to make you talk.

OK, if no one confesses, I'll punish all of you.

Don't tell me the dog did it.

I know one of you did it, and I'm going to find out who.

I'll leave no stone unturned in my search for truth.

And if I ever find out, you'll get what for.

THE MARTYR

I gave them the best years of my life...and
what thanks do I get?

Being a mother is a rotten job, but someone has to do it.

So far, no one else has volunteered.

A mother's work is never done.

There's never a dull moment.

If it's not one thing, it's another.

I can't get any peace and quiet.

It's so noisy around here, I can't hear myself think.

You don't even let me alone when I'm in the bathroom.

If you're trying to drive me crazy, you're too late.

I didn't get this gray hair at the beauty parlor.

Rodney Dangerfield's not the only one who can't get no respect.

You don't know how good you have it—no worries, no mortgage, and no taxes.

Just wait till you have kids of your own.

You'll be the death of me yet.

SECTION III:
AROUND THE HOUSE

THE HOUSEKEEPER

If you don't want to eat it, you can wear it.

What a mess.

There are more clothes on the floor than in your closet.

Apparently word of the invention of the laundry basket has not reached these parts.

What happened to the floor? I can't find it.

When was the last time you made your bed?

Your room looks like a tornado went through it.

Or a bomb hit it.

It should be declared a federal disaster area.

It's disgusting. How can you stand it?

You should be ashamed of yourself.

I'd be embarrassed to let anyone see this room.

Well, don't just sit there, start cleaning.

Don't expect me to clean it up. This isn't a hotel, and I'm not a chambermaid.

As long as you live under my roof, you'll keep your room neat and tidy.

OK, go ahead and live like a pig. See if I care.

But if you wake up one night and trip on your way to the bathroom, don't come crying to me.

And if your girlfriend finds out you're a slob and breaks up with you, don't say I didn't warn you.

Remember to keep your door shut at all times so I don't have to look at that mess.

If you ever leave your door open, I'll call the Salvation Army to haul all your stuff away.

THE HOME
ECONOMIST

Shut up. We're saving money for your college education.

Waste not, want not.

Close the front door; we can't heat the whole neighborhood.

Doesn't anyone know how to turn out a light in this house?

If I had a nickel for every time you left the lights on, I'd be a millionaire.

Don't stand there with the refrigerator door open.

Do you think we're made out of money?

You kids are going to send us to the poorhouse.

A penny saved is a penny earned.

You can't buy anything with a penny anymore. You might as well give it to "Jerry's kids."

You can't make a phone call for a dime anymore.

You can't buy a cup of coffee for a quarter, either.

A dollar doesn't go as far as it used to. It won't even buy you a ride on a dirty, smelly, unsafe, New York subway.

The best things in life are free—if you're a bird.

I may not wear the pants in this family, but I do pay the bills.

The only way I can pay my Visa bill this month is with my MasterCard.

THE DOCTOR

If you don't want to be 3 feet tall for
the rest of your life, drink your milk.

I'm cold; put on a sweater.

Always wear a scarf, or you'll catch your death of a cold.

Wear a hat whenever you're outside. I read in the newspaper that you lose 90 percent of your body heat through your head.

Feed a cold, starve a fever. Or is it starve a cold, feed a fever? I forget.

My chicken soup can cure anything.

But a little medicine wouldn't hurt, either.

Medicine's supposed to taste bad.

The worse it tastes, the better it is for you.

Do you want to stay sick? OK, stop complaining and take the medicine.

Would you mind throwing your used tissues in the garbage instead of on the floor?

Turn on the TV and find a funny show. No one ever died laughing.

Drink a glass of hot milk and get a good night's sleep—you'll feel a lot better in the morning.

I'd give you a good night kiss, but I don't want to catch whatever caught you.

When you're young, time will cure everything.

And when you're old, time will kill you.

THE BEAUTY CONSULTANT

This scale must be broken—and if it isn't broken,
I'm going to break it.

You look like something the cat dragged in.

Brush your hair; it looks like a rat's nest.

How much longer are you going to let your hair grow?

You have so much makeup on you look like a tramp.

If you bite your fingernails any shorter, you won't have any.

Beauty isn't only skin deep.

It would help if you didn't eat so much chocolate.

Have another piece of my apple pie.

Wear black; you'll look thinner.

Don't wear horizontal stripes; they make you look fat.

Maybe it's time you went on a diet.

You can't get by on looks alone.

Pretty is as pretty does.

If you walk like a queen, you'll feel like a queen.

Put this book on your head and walk across the room.

Beauty is in the eye of the beholder.

You may not be Miss America, but I think you're beautiful.

SECTION IV:
UNSOLICITED ADVICE

THE
CHEERLEADER

You were the most beautiful baby in the hospital.

If you weren't my baby, I would have taken you home anyway.

I'm lucky to have a child as wonderful as you.

No one will ever love you as much as your mother.

You have a lot to be thankful for.

You may not be a movie star, but baby—you've got what it takes.

You can do anything if you put your mind to it.

You should be happy. These are the best years of your life.

Just direct your feet to the sunny side of the street.

Don't make a mountain out of a molehill.

You have nothing to worry about—except for the permanent wrinkles on your forehead you'll have if you keep frowning.

Forget your troubles; come on, get happy.

Don't worry, be happy.

The only people without problems live in cemeteries.

No matter what happens, you can always come home to Mama.

THE MANNERS
PATROL

On this planet, we chew our food before we swallow it.

Mind your p's and q's.

"Please," "thank you," and "excuse me" are magic words.

Children should be seen and not heard.

Don't make a face or it'll freeze that way.

Don't cross your eyes or they'll stay crossed.

Don't stare or your eyeballs will get stuck.

Don't stick out your tongue or you'll trip over it.

Don't hang our dirty laundry out for everyone to see.

Don't interrupt me when I'm talking on the telephone.

Don't blow your own horn or you'll get an earache.

Don't talk with food in your mouth.

Don't chew gum with your mouth open. You look like a cow chewing its cud.

Don't use your sleeve for a handkerchief.

Don't slouch or your backbone will grow crooked.

If you can't say something nice, don't say anything at all.

Don't call me "she"; I'm your mother.

If you ever say that again, I'll wash your mouth out with soap.

Were you born in a barn?

What will the neighbors think?

You're just like your father.

You didn't learn your manners from my side of the family.

THE MORALIST

Cheating does *not* make the game more fun.

The trouble with trouble is that it starts out as fun.

Just say no to drugs.

Just say no to sex.

But don't you ever say no to me.

A clear conscience is a soft pillow.

Always tell the truth, and you'll never have to worry about your memory.

Honesty is the best policy.

Virtue is its own reward.

Actions speak louder than words.

Don't do anything you'll regret later.

The ends don't justify the means.

The road to hell is paved with good intentions.

Idle hands are the devil's workshop.

See no evil. Hear no evil. Speak no evil.

Remember, God is watching everything you do.

And He'll tell Santa Claus.

THE SOCIAL
DIRECTOR

You have to get along; you're sisters.

No man is an island.

He who seeks a friend without a fault will never find one.

A friend in need is a friend indeed.

If you want to make a friend, be a friend.

Share and share alike.

One good turn deserves another.

Always remember the golden rule.

Do unto others as you would have them do unto you.

It is better to suffer a wrong than to do a wrong.

Two wrongs don't make a right.

It is better to forgive than to fight.

You can catch more flies with honey than with vinegar.

To belittle is to be little.

Tact is the ability to shut your mouth before someone shuts it for you.

People who live in glass houses shouldn't throw stones.

Sticks and stones may break your bones, but names will never hurt you.

Nothing annoys your enemies so much as forgiving them.

If you lie down with dogs, you'll rise up with fleas.

And if you rise up with fleas, pretty soon you won't have any friends.

THE DATING ADVISOR

It's just a crush, dear; you'll get over it.

Don't worry, there are lots of good fish in the sea.

If you're looking for the perfect man, go to the movies.

Someday your prince will come. In the meantime, finish your homework.

How well do you know this guy who asked you to the prom?

Don't worry, he's probably just as nervous as you are.

Make sure you tell him how nice he looks.

Don't do anything I wouldn't do. I mean before I was married.

It's better to go dutch. The more he spends on a date, the more he expects after the date.

If he tries anything funny, call me on the telephone. And if there's no phone nearby, come right home.

If God had wanted you to fool around, He would have given us the Ten Suggestions.

Some men think of nothing but sex. And some men think of nothing.

Get your mind out of the gutter.

Be prepared. Odds are, he isn't.

It's better to be safe than sorry.

They say that love is blind. That's why men have such busy hands.

Men seldom make passes at female smartasses.

You have to chase him until he catches you.

No man will buy a cow if he can get the milk for free.

The reason smart women make foolish choices is that they don't listen to their mothers.

THE CONSOLER

I'll bet most of your friends would have been
happy to get a B+ in calculus.

Every cloud has a silver lining.

You're not overweight, you're big-boned.

You're not fat, you're pleasantly plump.

You're not short, you're petite.

Your nose isn't too big. Pretty soon the rest of your face will grow and you'll look just fine.

Your hair isn't red, it's auburn.

They may laugh at your braces now, but in a few years when your teeth are straight you'll have the last laugh.

You're lucky to be flat-chested; when you're sixty you won't sag into your soup.

I'd trade my gray hair for your acne in a minute.

Don't worry if you can't get a date—I think you're very nice.

So you're not a social butterfly—you're a late bloomer.

I never dated when I was in high school. Come to think of it, I didn't date much in college, either.

It may hurt now, but just remember: bees die right after they sting you.

If at first you don't succeed, you're like most people.

Winning isn't everything.

It doesn't matter whether you win or lose—as long as you have a good time.

You might have come in last, but at least you finished the race.

You're not the first person who ever flunked calculus, and you won't be the last.

There are lots of things in life worse than forgetting your only line in the school play.

You're bound to be good at something. You just don't know what it is yet.

THE WORRIER

What will the neighbors think?

An ounce of prevention is worth a pound of cure.

A stitch in time saves nine.

It's better to leave well enough alone.

There's always a calm before the storm.

Make haste slowly.

Look before you leap.

He who hesitates is lost.

It's better to be safe than sorry.

But it's better to be sorry than dead.

He who lives by the sword, dies by the sword.

Might doesn't make right, but it does start a fight.

He who fights and runs away, lives to fight another day.

Live and let live.

If it's not broken, don't fix it.

Don't tinker with success.

In fact, don't tinker at all.

Don't count your chickens before they hatch.

Don't put all your eggs in one basket.

Don't bite off more than you can chew.

Be careful what you wish for—you might get it.

THE SAGE

Enjoy yourself—it's later than you think.

Pride goeth before a fall.

The pot shouldn't call the kettle black.

Everything in moderation.

Too much of a good thing can be dangerous.

It's better to light a candle than to curse the darkness.

You can't have your cake and eat it, too.

You can lead the horse to water, but you can't make it drink.

What goes around, comes around.

Someday your chickens will come home to roost.

The ripest peach is the highest on the tree.

You can't turn back the clock. But you can wind it up again.

You can never be too skinny or too rich.

When the going gets tough, the tough go shopping.

Don't throw the baby out with the bathwater.

Don't cut off your nose to spite your face.

Don't burn your candle at both ends.

Don't judge a book by its cover.

Why is life so tough? Maybe it's been cooked too long.

TV MOMS COUCH POTATO QUIZ

Test your knowledge of the "wit and wisdom" of TV moms. Try to match the TV mom with her quote. The correct answers are listed on the next page. A perfect score means you're a perfect couch potato.

1. Roseanne
   "Roseanne"

2. Elyse Keaton
   "Family Ties"

3. June Cleaver
   "Leave It to Beaver"

4. Lucy
   "I Love Lucy"

5. Marion Cunningham
   "Happy Days"

6. Peg Bundy
   "Married...with Children"

7. Carol Brady
   "The Brady Bunch"

8. Edith Bunker
   "All in the Family"

9. Claire Huxtable
   "The Cosby Show"

10. Marge Simpson
    "The Simpsons"

a. "Child, don't talk to your mother that way."

b. "Oh my!"

c. "OK, who's going to help me make the tofu tacos?"

d. "Before your father and I were married, we hardly ever watched TV."

e. "Ah, shut up!"

f. "We have a problem—it's called the generation gap."

g. "Waaaaaah!"

h. "I love it when you're frisky."

i. "You actually want me to cook you dinner?"

j. "Boys, go wash up for dinner."

Answers on next page.

97

ANSWERS

1. e	6. i
2. c	7. f
3. j	8. b
4. g	9. a
5. h	10. d

Dads Say the Dumbest Things!
by Bruce Lansky and Ken Jones

Lansky and Jones have collected all the greatest lines dads have ever used to get kids to stop fighting in the car, feed the pet, turn off the TV while doing their homework, and get home before curfew from a date. It includes such winners as: "What do you want a pet for—you've got a sister" and "When I said 'feed the goldfish,' I didn't mean feed them to the cat." A fun gift for dad.
Order #4220

Italian Without Words
by Don Cangelosi and Joseph Delli Carpini

Now you can visit Italy and order a meal, make a date, curse like a trooper, or make intimidating threats without knowing a single word of Italian. This ingenious Italian "phrase book" contains the most common gestures and body language, so you can speak like an Italian without spending a fortune at Berlitz. It must be seen to be believed!
Order #5100

Grandma Knows Best,
But No One Ever Listens
by Mary McBride

Mary McBride offers much-needed advice for new grandmas on how to
- Show baby photos to anyone, any time
- Get out of babysitting...or if stuck, to housebreak the kids before they wreck the house
- Advise the daughter-in-law without being banned from her home.

The perfect gift for grandma, Phyllis Diller says it's "harder to put down than a new grandchild."
Order #4009

Order Form

Quantity	Title	Author	Order No.	Unit Cost	Total
	Baby & Child Medical Care	Hart, T.	1159	$8.00	
	Baby Name Personality Survey, The	Lansky/Sinrod	1270	$7.00	
	Best Baby Name Book, The	Lansky, B.	1029	$5.00	
	Best Baby Shower Book, The	Cooke, C.	1239	$6.00	
	Birth Partner's Handbook, The	Jones, C.	1309	$6.00	
	Dads Say the Dumbest Things!	Lansky/Jones	4220	$6.00	
	David, We're Pregnant!	Johnston, L.	1049	$6.00	
	Discipline W/out Shouting/ Spanking	Wyckoff/Unell	1079	$6.00	
	Do They Ever Grow Up?	Johnston, L.	1089	$6.00	
	Feed Me! I'm Yours	Lansky, V.	1109	$8.00	
	First-Year Baby Care	Kelly, P.	1119	$7.00	
	Free Stuff for Kids, 1992 Edition	FS Editors	2190	$5.00	
	Getting Organized for Your New Baby	Bard, M.	1229	$5.00	
	Grandma Knows Best	McBride, M.	4009	$5.00	
	Hi, Mom! Hi, Dad!	Johnston, L.	1139	$6.00	
	Italian Without Words	Cangelosi/Carpini	5100	$5.00	
	It's My Party	Croasdale/Davis	2390	$5.95	
	Kids Pick the Funniest Poems	Lansky, B.	2410	$13.00	
	Moms Say the Funniest Things!	Lansky, B.	4280	$6.00	
	Mother Murphy's Law	Lansky, B.	1149	$4.50	
	Pregnancy, Childbirth, and the Newborn	Simkin/Whalley/Keppler	1169	$12.00	
	Ready for School?	Eberts/Gisler	1360	$5.95	
	Visualizations for an Easier Childbirth	Jones, C.	1330	$6.00	
	Working Woman's Guide to Breastfeeding	Dana/Price	1259	$7.00	
				Subtotal	
			Shipping and Handling (see below)		
			MN residents add 6.5% sales tax		
				Total	

YES! Please send me the books indicated above. Add $1.50 shipping and handling for the first book and $.50 for each additional book. Add $2.00 to total for books shipped to Canada. Overseas postage will be billed. Allow up to 4 weeks for delivery. Send check or money order payable to Meadowbrook Press. No cash or C.O.D.'s, please. Prices subject to change without notice. **Quantity discounts available upon request.**

Name _____ Phone _____

Address _____

City _____ State _____ Zip _____.___

☐ Check or money order payable to Meadowbrook (No cash or C.O.D.'s, please.)
Amount enclosed $_____

☐ Visa (for orders over $10 only.)   ☐ MasterCard (for orders over $10 only.)
Account # _____

Signature _____ Exp. Date _____

You can also phone us for orders of $10.00 or more at 1-800-338-2232.

A *FREE* Meadowbrook Press catalog is available upon request.

Meadowbrook, Inc., 18318 Minnetonka Boulevard, Deephaven, Minnesota 55391
(612) 473-5400   Toll-Free 1-800-338-2232   Fax (612) 475-0736